Write Your First Book

in 30 Days

Revised 2018

First Published in the U.S. by Copper Canopy Press
Copyright © Christina Dreve Young 2017
Edited by Jonny Bahk-Hahlberg

ISBN-13: 978-0-9967760-8-0

copper
canopy
press

www.coppercanopypress.com

Write Your First Book in 30 Days

Get Ready,
Get Support,
and Get Writing!

CHRISTINA DREVE YOUNG

For You, Dear Reader,

That you may recover your dreams, release your fears, and

write the book that only you can write.

Contents

Part I

Get Ready to Write

Introduction

While it may only take an hour to read this book, I spent four years testing this approach to writing. Now you can also write your first book in just 30 days. You'll get the practical steps to develop your characters and create your plot, and understand how to think about writing before you type the first word. If you can absorb the key concepts, this step-by-step process will even help you enjoy the writing process. At the end of one month, you'll have a terrific working manuscript, and you'll be happy about your work.

There are two popular theories about writing; you can outline the whole book ahead of time, or you can just let words fly out and see what happens. If you were heading to the grocery store, would you make a list of ingredients for the next 3 days of cooking, or do you just wander the aisles and see what jumps into your cart?

We know from experience that when you plan your purchases, you usually have delicious meals. The hardest part is the preparation time. I wish dinner would magically assemble itself, get cooked, and land in a pile of steamy deliciousness on my plate. This book will help you actually prepare a feast of words, and assemble them into an appealing story!

While this will direct you to the core of your story, it's only the start. The fun part is pulling the individual pieces together to make a book. If you want to have a successful month of novel or memoir writing, you need to prepare yourself. Part of that is the emotional commitment to sit in your chair and write every day. If you want a crappy first draft, then plan on 30 minutes a day. If you want to write something that has potential to be shaped into a published novel, you need to plan on 60 to 90 minutes a day. And that's usually why people don't *ever* write their books. They simply won't sit down and write. It sounds obvious, I know, but if you want to write a book, you have to spend time writing.

There are a few other reasons people never write their book...

- they think they should spend years writing it
- they should wait until they retire to write it
- or, they think they don't have the skill to put a story onto paper.

You may worry about spelling, or grammar, or fret about the proper way to assemble a sentence. Maybe you've heard stories from others who are "writing a book", and have been for years. If you think you should wait until you have time to write a book, that means you've got some residual bad programming from your school days. It's no reflection on you. School was partly designed to make us stand in lines and be obedient. Writing a book completely contradicts those lessons. While we can still be proud of our diplomas, we didn't always get the encouragement needed to develop our creativity. School did not applaud our originality, and being unique further separated us from the other kids our age.

Even now that you're a grown-up, you may still doubt your skills and talents. We will address mindset in this book, because even the best advice in the world won't help if you don't sit in your chair and write. Following these steps will let you finally share your story. It's okay that you don't know every detail yet. The important thing is your driving need to put your creative self to work, and I am here to support you. Let's get started!

Getting Ready

There are a few things you can do to make this easier on yourself. Do you have a desk? A computer? Pencils and notepaper? A lamp? A door you can close, or headphones you can put on?

Even if you have a designated writing studio, you have to set it up to optimize your writing time. You cannot answer emails when you write. (Close your email program.) You can't think about your bills when you write. (Keep a notepad handy so you can jot down those intrusive thoughts and deal with them later.) And you have to allow yourself to stay focused on your writing, which means sitting in your chair for 33 minutes at a time. Have a big glass of water ready and take care of biological functions before you sit down. There's no reason to leave your chair in your 33-minute writing block.

Why 33 minutes? First, because it seems like an achievable goal. If you can sit and watch a movie every now and then, you can certainly sit down and write for 33 minutes. Even if you DO have to a biological urge, most people can hold it that long! If you know you can quit after 33 minutes, then it's an easy commitment. When the kitchen timer goes off, you stop writing mid-sentence. (That's correct, no cell phones are to be used for a timer. *This is your sacred writing time, and nothing shall interrupt you*.) The next two minutes are for jumping jacks, getting more coffee, or if you prefer, screaming into a pillow. After being refreshed, spend just 33 more minutes writing. You have to give yourself time to get into the flow of creativity. Let yourself get in to the story, imagine colors, places, and people, and let that come through your fingertips.

The reason for the exact time of 33 minutes is a copywriting trick from the master of advertising, Gene Schwartz. His rule was to sit down to work for 33 minutes. He could choose to stare at the wall, drink his coffee, or write. No matter which activity he chose, he stayed there for his promised time. Schwartz went on a blue streak of a career, churning out one brilliant campaign after another, because he made himself do it. He let no excuse stop him.

Since I've been spending 33-minute blocks at my keyboard, I've successfully completed seven books. This was even before I learned to touch type, and my "production rate" was 1500 words in half an hour. When I did fail at a thirty-day sprint, it was because I didn't plan what I was going to write ahead of time.

When I had to stop in the middle of a sentence at the 33-minute mark, I knew exactly where I would start writing tomorrow. It meant I was returning to a story in progress instead of a blank new chapter. You'll be amazed at the drive you have to get back and finish that section.

The other key to success for me was setting an appointment time to write. I'm a morning person, so I set my alarm for 5:20 a.m. I grabbed a cup of coffee, and went to my laptop immediately. The house was quiet, and I admit I felt a little superior that I'd done my bit of writing for the day before most people were awake. Just pay attention to your own body clock, find your energy peak, and try to write during that time.

Prerequisites for Writing

In order to write a first draft in thirty days, there are some basic things you need to have, and things you'll agree to do. Otherwise, this is not a good time to write your first book. Here they are:

- Own a computer with a keyboard
- Either own Microsoft Word, have access to Google Docs, or own a word processing program called Scrivener. ($40 for a lifetime license, also available for a free 30 day trial at www.literatureandlatte.com)
- You've looked at your schedule and you're willing to change your commitments drastically to make room for writing
- You're willing to give up social media, TV shows, and helping other people for the next thirty days. (This one is important! You can use your witty comebacks and cleverly posted content in your book. Don't squander that on a news feed!)
- Tip - try out the "unschedule" at http://www.neilfiore.com/now-habit-schedules/ to find time to write
- Promise that you will write a first draft without stopping or editing, and you won't backspace or erase anything that you write for the next 30 days.
- Make a public declaration that you will write a novel in 30 days. Post on social media ahead of time, and tell

everyone you know about your plans. They may think you're a little nuts, but that's okay. Many of those same people will encourage you, support you, and even admire your crazy goal.

If these foundational pieces are in place, you'll give yourself more than a chance at writing your first book. All that's left is time at the keyboard.

What is a First Draft?

How will I ever put my thoughts on to paper?

This is something that will happen naturally when you spend time writing. If you don't sit yourself in that seat for 33-99 minutes a day, I promise that nothing will happen. Once you allow your creativity to flow, there is no telling the wonders you'll encounter. Characters start to take actions you never imagined, and say things you've never heard someone say in real life. They will only do this if you give them the time they need to develop.

Here's the really hard part…writing without getting up from your seat, writing without looking something up on the Internet, and re-reading what you've already written. Those three things will absolutely kill your productivity. There's no doubt, and no question about it. If you have any hope of writing this book, you must not open a browser window during your writing time. No matter how strong the need to look up the name of a lizard species that is mostly yellow, DO NOT DO IT. Instead, write that sentence in italics, all capital letters, or underline it. Do something that will direct you back to that spot after your first draft is written. I cannot state this strongly enough. You will completely sabotage yourself if you switch to research mode during your writing time. Got it?

As far as re-reading goes, that's also a "no-no". Okay, you can read the last few sentences where you left off if you must, but don't go back any further than that. You simply don't have the time on this tight deadline to reminisce. (Or form an opinion of the quality of your writing so far.) Just allow yourself a little time and distance, and stay on track to create more words on paper. There is time to edit later. Okay?

Staying planted in your seat for small chunks of writing time is the foundation of the entire writing process. If you have to sit at the computer and just cry, do that for your writing time. When the timer goes off, you can get a tissue. In the meantime, use your sleeve.

Now is the time to decide your writing chunks. Will you go 33 minutes, stop in the middle of a sentence, and then take a two-minute break before your next block? Will you sit there for 45 minutes and then be done for the day? You have to have a plan. Remember that this is only for 30 days, and then you can be as distracted and skittish as you want. Right now, you must create. You can only create when you're sitting at the keyboard. Don't lie to yourself and say you can jot ideas down from your dreams, and then just spend ten minutes typing up your next chapter. You're cheating yourself of an incredible opportunity to WRITE A BOOK. So do what you've committed to do; sit in your chair and write.

It's easiest if you write from your heart. Act as if you were talking to a friend. Don't think you have to write like Shakespeare or anyone else you've ever read. Don't try to make it "fancy" or perfect, because you'll just freeze up from all the pressure. Just be yourself. It reminds me of a quote attributed to Gilbert Perreira: "Be yourself, everyone else is already taken."

But I'm Not a Writer…

Writing a book is not the same as a school writing assignment. There's no right answer, and there are no guidelines on what you should write. This is something of your own invention, and coming up with ideas can sometimes be a challenge. When you try to use writing methods from your school days, you will multiply your difficulties.

With a specific subject for an assigned essay, you would think of your opening sentence, tumble it around in your head to make it better, and only then would you then type it. Does that seem about right? This line of thinking is why everyone is afraid of the blank page, and why they don't know where to start. School training is coming back to haunt us!

It is uncommon (actually, it's impossible) to write something perfectly the first time. If you think you can, that's another flashback moment from your school days. We are programmed to become defensive when we are corrected. Because only "dummies" are called out in front of their classmates.

Let me ask you about the last time someone approached you with a concern or complaint. What was your initial reaction? Was it calm and thoughtful, or did you feel a burst of shame or anger?

I am going to blame our school system for creating that either/or dichotomy in our thinking, especially in thinking about ourselves. In school there are two choices; right or wrong, and there's no gray area of behavior. You were either a good kid, or a troublemaker. That way of thinking is also attached to the subjects we learned in school. If I tell you that **no one** writes a good first draft, your natural reflex is to disagree, and tell me you are a good kid. You **can** write a good first draft.

I want you to try it my way this time, because you are a grown-up now.

There is amazing freedom that comes when we don't pressure ourselves. It sounds kind of obvious when you re-read that last sentence, but realizing the harm that school has done to your thinking is really important. People tell me all the time they failed English, they were a C student, or that they aren't creative. We are all creative. Even my first cousin, who lives in a group home because of his mental challenges, is an artist. The real problem is when we judge the quality of our creativity, and then decide our art is no good.

The bottom line is that you have to let yourself practice. You have to spend time in your chair writing. Try just writing whatever comes into your head, then immediately write the next sentence. Don't stop to re-read, just go ahead and write the next sentence. And the next. If you want to write a book, you have to put words onto the page. Don't judge yourself yet. Save that for the editing time after you've written your first draft. You will never finish your draft if you let your student mindset rule your writing time. You are good enough. You are creative. And yes, you are a writer.

In school, we studied all the great authors; George Orwell, Maya Angelou, Mark Twain, and more. Schooling uses the model of models, showing you the ideal outcome, the perfect example. It's meant to show us our end goal. As children, we don't have the experience yet to create our own perfect work. School is a time of practice and correction, and our western system of teaching is to ingrain those models into our imagination.

Unless you've spent a lot of time writing for "fun" since then, this idea of perfection is deeply seated in your subconscious. It makes you believe that you cannot write, and makes you run from the label of writer. What was meant to be helpful in school now harms your ability to create. Can you see that? Now that you are an adult, it's time to allow yourself that writing time. Let yourself practice, and put some words down on paper.

When I first became a writing coach, I was terrified to read the work of my clients. I knew they would ask for my feedback, and I was concerned it would be terrible. What would I say to them? Would I be that mean teacher who judged her students?

The truth is that beautiful things happen when we follow our instincts. When we stop judging ourselves and let the creativity flow through us, we find writing enjoyable. We become drawn into the stories we are creating, and they begin to live on their own. Characters consume our thoughts, and part of our imagination starts to live in the story all the time. Our dreams become lucid, our intuition heightens, and we enjoy the process of writing.

We even claim the label of writer for ourselves. When you can let go of perfection long enough to let yourself write, you will become a writer too.

I'm Too Busy to Write a Book

Yes, we are all busy. We add things to our schedule just to stay in constant motion. Sometimes I feel like busy-ness means I'm "important", and if I don't have commitments every hour of every day, I'm either lazy or unpopular. Is it just me who thinks that way?

Sometimes my clients tell me they don't have thirty minutes a day to write. Really? People somehow find time to watch their favorite shows, pursue hobbies, and keep their laundry clean. I've certainly watched my share of Netflix. (In fact, I just ended my subscription because I was getting too addicted to on-demand series!)

Writing a book is not a chore. It's not an obligation. It should feel like a fun and exciting project, full of promise and potential. When you know this is a limited 30-day time commitment that will result in a book, it's worth the time spent.

Be honest with yourself about the 24 hours you have each day. For a three-day period, check in hourly to see what you've accomplished. Of course, your job is a requirement, and hopefully you enjoy your time there as well. Just observe your choices, and don't judge yourself for them. There's a reason you do what you do. It could be because you have kids and a household to run. Maybe you do something because you've always done it, and now it's simply a habit. Take three days to notice how you might choose to use some of that time to write.

If you've decided that you are ready for your first book, here's how to create the ideal conditions for your writing project.

First, you have to designate an actual writing space. It could be an office, a desk in the corner of your bedroom, or an end table by your couch. Preferably, it needs to stay in the same place for the next thirty days. This also needs to be a place you can focus on word production. If there are stacks of distractions (like bills to be paid, books to read, or children to feed), this is not the best place to write.

The time of day can also affect your production… If you can rise early and get to the computer while your family sleeps, all the better. If you are a night owl, tuck them all in, and get to your writing space.

Writing at the same time each day for the next thirty days is essential. Not only will you program yourself to be productive in your short writing time, it also allows full recovery and maximum hours between writing sessions. You can do anything for just thirty days, right?

When you sit down to the computer, disconnect yourself from the Internet and email. You don't want social media alerts popping up, or inbox messages to take you off flow. This little chunk of writing time is a real gift if you let yourself have it. You will be amazed and impressed with what you can do when you let yourself focus!

Keep some note cards or a legal pad next to your computer as you write. Sometimes those to-do items pop into your head and won't leave you alone. When that happens, write it on the paper next to you. Your survival brain now sees that you will take care of that need, and you'll be able to get back to writing. Try it, it works.

I also suggest a writing "ritual". This is how you can create a tangible space for yourself that confirms that you are doing something special and out-of-the-ordinary. Take a few deep breaths before you begin. Let go of all your daily tasks, and just focus on your writing time. You can even dress up in a little writing costume! Wear a hat or a bandana around your neck, throw something over your shoulders, or wear your favorite smoking jacket. These are all signals to your subconscious that you are doing something different. If you think you are too mature for this, I encourage you to try a little silliness, even if it's for 33 minutes a day!

Surround yourself with things you like. Create a spot near you for rocks, statues, or whatever inspires you. Your writing space should feel special. Because something special will happen when you spend time there, letting yourself write!

Plotting Out Your Book

To write a first draft in 30 days, use this three-step plan. First, you need to have characters. Second is the setting for your story. Finally, you'll create the plot points, also known as the story line.

I use a spiral bound, wide-ruled notebook to plan each new book. Start on the back of page two, and write the character's name on the left hand page. You'll end up with facing pages for each character's description, or the "back story" for your character. This is your cast of characters, and where you develop their individual personalities. You'll probably have ideas you don't get to use in the book, but when you write about them, their unspoken traits will still shine through.

In this section, note what they look like, how they talk, what they wear, and other aspects of their personality. You can add quirky traits, how they limp, or some of their favorite catch phrases. Also include their family and love relationships, their age, and other statistical information. Think of this as an FBI case file. You need the facts collected in one place.

Once you begin writing, you'll be surprised at the need to look things up about your character. I've even used my character notebook to be sure I was using the correct name!

Leave some extra pages after you've listed your main characters. You'll be adding incidental players that need to be invented during your writing process.

That one blank page at the front will become your index, created as you sketch out your characters and settings. You can add your own page numbers in the top right corner of the right hand pages. I find it easiest to just number those, rather than every single page, and the top corner is not usually covered with writing.

After the characters, make a page for locations. Where do you imagine your scenes taking place? What season is it, and does your story occur in the present day? Write out a page for each setting, and what you imagine will happen there. Use descriptive words so your setting evokes emotion.

Describe how that room looks, what kind of furniture is there, and what you'd see from the window. Is it carpeted? Is it warm? How do you feel in that room? You are creating a vignette, much like a set builder does for a play. You want the mood of those places to contribute to the action in each scene.

This pre-work helps you place yourself in the story, and think about what will happen. Writing your novel is easier when you've already imagined your story coming to life. Doing this little bit of planning creates wonderful momentum, and gets you excited to write.

After you list your scenes and characters, it's much easier to add your story line. I like to use a large piece of craft paper and sketch out a messy mind map. You can buy actual butcher paper, or just get a roll of heavy-duty wrapping paper and write on the back of it. This set-up allows you to add, erase, and re-arrange your story as needed. You can use colored pencils or a number 2 pencil. I never use ink pens for this part because I always end up re-arranging the map. Using circles to enclose your ideas lets you zoom out to a macro level, and get the bird's eye view of your story.

This also encourages you to start in the middle, and add the beginning later. It's intimidating to face the blank page, and writing a novel presents that same challenge. People ask me how they should start their book, thinking they should start at the very beginning. (Remember "Do Re Mi" from the Sound of Music? I think we have that song absorbed into our thinking!)

However, I tell them to start with the scene that most excites them, the one they cannot wait to write. It could be the high point of your story, or even the resolution.

Just keep adding ideas and circles to your map until you have a beginning, middle, and end. This is the easiest way to plan your book. I've also used Nigel Watts' eight-point story arc that includes stasis, trigger, quest, surprise, critical choice, climax, reversal, and resolution. If you need more help designing your plot, you can use the Hero's Journey (by Joseph Campbell) as your guide. Search online for that one. Also, look up Christopher Vogler's distilled version with 12 steps.

If you're a visual person, search online for "plot outline" in the "image" results. Browse through and find something that makes sense to you, and start with that structure. I could tell you there's one right answer to plot planning, but we know there's never one right answer for anything in life. Writing is as individual as a fingerprint, and everyone will find their own best way.

However, planning is crucial for *everyone*, no matter how their plot is structured. It's the heart of your story. Once that's in place, you can start to fill in the rest. Post your story map on the wall near your writing space so you don't forget anything. Although you plan to write your story in one short month, you will still need to refer to your map and notebook. Use these tools to help you!

Write Now

To successfully write your book in 30 days, I suggest two weeks of prep time. These are your action items:

- Prepare your writing space
- Get the software you need
- Look at your schedule
- Make a public commitment
- Create your notebook with characters, places, and plot points

This little bit of planning will provide fertile ground for your writing. All you need to know right now is your cast of characters, and the general direction they're heading. You don't have to know every detail of your story before you begin. Once you start writing, your characters will make their own decisions. This may sound weird to you, but it's one of my favorite surprises every time. The creative process is strangely thrilling, and what I end up writing is more fun than I ever could have planned.

Next, you have to choose a 30-day writing period. I find that starting on the first day of the month is more natural than starting in the middle. Now you'll decide which time of day you'll write, and how long you'll write each day. Will you take Sundays off, or write every day for 30 days in a row? Talk to your friends and family, and explain the time commitment you're making to your first draft. Gently explain you will not be available for the activities you've decided to sacrifice for the month. Remind them you're only writing for 30 days, then you'll be back better than ever. Explain how satisfied you'll be to have written the book you've wanted to write. You finally did this for yourself!

Spend a little more time with character development. Carry a smaller notebook (or index cards) with you at all times for the next two weeks. When an idea pops into your head, write it down. You'll think you can remember it, but please be kind to your creativity and jot it down. You can even dictate an email to yourself on your smartphone if you wish. (I recommend against voice memos, because that requires going back and transcribing.)

Do you know how to touch type? I resisted learning this, but it was a huge help to my word production. Somehow, I signed up for the nine key calculator class in high school instead of typing. (If you don't know what that is, let me say I can total math problems with amazing speed and accuracy without looking at the keyboard.)

To learn to touch type, I bought a Mavis Beacon software program designed for kids. I figured I might "game-ify" my learning process, then give the CD to my nieces when I was finished. It worked. Sometimes I still backslide to using seven of my ten available digits on the keyboard, but the time I gained from backspacing was invaluable.

That's almost everything you need to do to get ready to write. There is one last thing to address, and it's a bit touchy.

If you want to bounce your ideas off of someone, don't use your spouse or best buddies. If you do happen to have an exceptionally creative circle of friends, then go ahead and use them. When I was an aspiring writer, I didn't find much support close at hand. People just didn't get me, and it was crushing to my creativity. But I don't want you to keep your ideas a secret either. Just be aware of who you talk to, and know that you may not find the feedback you were hoping for.

I can tell you that accountability has been a huge part of my writing success. Simply telling someone that I was writing a book made it easier. Once I added to my circle (beyond friends and family,) I felt supported in my writing. I actually hired a coach to help me figure out that I was a writer. Maybe that seems extreme to you, but that primal creative force inside was scary. Perhaps you can relate to that, or maybe you already embrace your identity as a writer. I still have a coach to this day, because I know I have a tendency toward inactivity, laziness, and Netflix series. It's a battle I think we all fight as human beings so I'm not ashamed to admit that.

Since becoming a writing coach myself, I also offer that support to my clients. It's been life changing to have a coach, and my clients tell me the same thing. It really is hard to find other people who understand who you are, and that you're driven to create. If you'd like to tell me about your book project, I'd be happy to set up a free forty-five-minute project discussion. Copy this link and let's chat: https://www.timetrade.com/book/MH971.

I wish you all the writing success you desire. Write Now!

Part II

Create Your Own 30-Day Writing Contest

What is National Novel Writing Month?

This is a contest that challenges you to write 50,000 in 30 days. You don't have to consider yourself a writer to try this. Since you can talk, you already know how to structure words into thoughts, and thoughts into sentences. It also doesn't have to take years to write your book. Reading this will get you ready to write a first draft in 30 days, even with only 30 minutes of daily writing time. You can participate in the official National Novel Writing Month (NaNoWriMo), which happens every November. You could also make this a personal contest, and set it up for any month that works with your schedule. If you follow this advice, you can have your first draft completed one short month from now. Take action and write the story you've been wanting to tell, instead of waiting for someday.

I wrote these tips as a result of failing at my first NaNoWriMo contest. Thinking I could just jump in with no preparation was my first mistake. Writing as I did in college was my second mistake. Editing as I wrote was the absolute worst thing I could have done. I needed to completely change my approach to writing if I ever wanted to write a book, let alone write it in 30 days.

Taking the next eleven months to research, I was driven to find the secret to writing 50,000 words *next* November. There were plenty of people who "won" the contest by hitting the word count goal. Clearly it was possible.

I read books about writing, I read more fiction and non-fiction, and practiced my journaling. I tried advice from different authors and started to figure it out. Coming from a family of teachers, I decided to lead a writer's group to test my ideas. I wound up with three groups on meetup.com; one for memoir, one for fiction, and one for business owners who wanted their book to get more clients.

Although the three groups had distinct differences, similarities also emerged. A framework began to show itself, and I created a step-by-step process that worked for everyone.

The biggest hurdle was breaking free of what we'd learned in school. Once my writers gave themselves permission to write *crap*, things changed. Let me explain...

Most of us don't call ourselves writers, and we don't think we're particularly creative. This stops us from attempting a book. I started asking my groups to write silly stuff they knew would never be published. They practiced putting words on a page, and they got better. They found out that writing poorly was the first step to writing well.

I developed a specific process that helped them feel better about writing, and let them prove they could do it. We talked about the process of writing, and built on small successes.

The techniques in this book will challenge what you think about writing. They will create a mindset of abundance, and prove there are no limits to your creativity. This book will help you honor the deep desire you have to write, and the desire you have for your writing to make a difference.

As you allow your ideas to surface, it can be uncomfortable. Writing is solitary, and requires that you turn inward to allow your true self to emerge. Because we spend so much time hiding from ourselves, avoiding our feelings, and wearing masks of self-protection, what we uncover in our writing can scare us. When we aren't familiar with the workings of our imagination, our first attempts at writing are "not normal" to us. By spending time writing, your thoughts will develop, and your writer's voice will emerge.

This is the writing that only you can do. It's tempting to write like you did when you were in school. However, taking that approach at this point will likely paralyze you. Since your school days you've lived a little (worked, traveled, and had friendships.) You have experiences that no one else has. Sure, you've shared events and circumstances with other people, but your lens of perspective is yours, and yours alone.

This is what I mean by the writer's voice. It's sharing how you see the world...how you interpret the events in your past, and how you felt about them. No one else sees things the same way you do.

When you use the safety net of these writing prompts, you can express the opinions that perhaps you're afraid of being judged for. Letting words fall onto the page is an important first step to becoming a real writer. Getting past self-judgment is the only way to do this.

You don't have to show your writing to anyone. Start out with that one simple promise to yourself. This is a special and sacred time, and the process of becoming a writer is delicate. Allow your creativity to take shape within this quiet and protected space. Nurture yourself, and treat your writing as a tender shoot breaking through the surface of the soil. The writing prompts are the rich fuel that will help you become rooted. Your writing time is the sunshine to strengthen your ideas.

First, you have to give yourself that gift of time at the keyboard. As you let your ideas emerge, you'll rediscover your unique perspective. Writing is the perfect way to express the message that only you can share.

Using these writing prompts will also make your writing enjoyable. Perhaps your last experience of writing was in school. Those essays were often written under pressure, and your goal was a good grade. Having an assigned topic boxed in your imagination, and ruled out creativity. Using the formula of the thesis sentence, and then supporting that thesis in your paragraph created the drive for perfect writing. While that concept is still important to your story flow, we're going to do something different here. Telling your story may be difficult, and releasing yourself from the pressure of perfection will make your first draft easier to write. It may even be fun!

If you don't enjoy writing, you shouldn't do it. My clients are always surprised when I tell them this. They have a burning story they want to tell about their addiction recovery, losing a loved one, or how they survived past hurts. There's no doubt that writing is therapeutic, but sometimes the stories we tell ourselves about our past become overwhelming when we think about writing them down.

This is completely normal.

By easing into your story with writing prompts, you will be reminded that you are strong and resilient. It's okay to see past hurts, and know you can choose what to write about now. Maybe you will never write *that* story, or maybe you will. Please remember that putting pressure on yourself will completely block your writing.

These prompts will support you through the process of self-discovery. They were carefully chosen, and placed in a specific order to build your confidence. These writing prompts will help you write without editing, and write a lot.

Allow yourself to try this method of writing. Promise yourself that no one will read it. Your feelings and opinions will safely emerge from their hidden places, and you will find your writer's voice.

How Could I Ever Write 1667 Words a Day?

When you do the math, you will "just" need to write 1667 words a day for thirty days to hit the 50K word count. You can do it by incorporating freewriting into your skill set. Freewriting means that every thought you have can be written down. This idea may seem crazy at first. As children, we learned we couldn't say everything we thought. In school, we learned those rules of writing and grammar.

In freewriting, you do not edit as you write. Simply fill a page with words. Ignore the rules, and let the child in you run wild!

You'll get the best results after warming up. If you only write for three minutes, you'll stop short of the truth. Instead, give yourself permission to play. Spend ten full minutes writing to move past those things that usually stop you. Your pen will naturally pause between thoughts, so keep moving by re-writing your last sentence. You could also write, "What's next?"

These pages are a safe place to write because there's no pressure. This is just an experiment you won't share with anyone. This process invites the unseen *you* into being. You don't have to keep up appearances as you write, and you don't have to make anyone else happy. In this place, you are free. As a collection of experiences and beliefs, you do have something to say! This process of freewriting will help you refine and polish your ideas.

Remember that writing prompts have no correct answer; take your personal expression wherever you wish. Maybe you'll write a personal essay, a poem, or a short story. Maybe a prompt will simply transform fuzzy thinking into a clear idea. Enjoy what happens when you stop censoring yourself. I once heard a poet explain that freewriting is like clearing her throat before a speech. We are on this adventure to make speeches, proclaim our stories, and share what we've discovered. This is the creative permission you've been waiting for! Find your writer's voice, get your head right, and you'll discover that you *are* a writer.

Write now.

Part III

Freewriting

How to Use Writing Prompts

This book is arranged to take you from your normal now, to writing the biggest and best life for yourself. Start at the beginning and explore each writing prompt in order. Allow your adventure to unfold in its own way. Your stories are there inside, waiting to emerge from your imagination. When you follow the suggested writing times listed for each section, you'll get the best results. Don't shortcut your creative process. Give yourself permission to write for those seven or ten minutes, and you will enjoy writing. I promise!

Ready? Let's write.

The Ultimate Vacation Spot

Imagine yourself with your car keys in hand as you head out the door. You get in and drive off, and two minutes down the road you see something intriguing. A factory is nearby, and you never paid attention to it before. The parking lot is huge, brightly lit, and empty. The lights are on inside.

You feel a pull towards the building, park the car, and walk up to the door. There's an elevator there and your initials are on the button. Curious and excited, you press the button and the doors slide open. Once inside, the panel again has only one button with your initials on it. You press the button and the front doors close, while the rear doors instantly open.

You look through the open elevator door into the space, and you're awestruck. You could not have designed a space any more perfect for yourself.

How did all of this get here? It's as if someone knew exactly what you wanted and needed, and created an incredible space for you to discover at precisely the right time in your life.

The air inside smells delightful and it's perfectly safe and inviting. You enter the space, amazed at this turn of events.

There is no obligation to stay, no cost or rent involved, and no clock anywhere to be seen. It is totally your choice to stay for however long you wish, and you are completely protected in this space.

Spend some time looking around, and discover what's here for you. When you're ready, let your thoughts flow onto the paper. Describe this the space that was created especially for you.

<Write for ten minutes>

Another Day of Normal

What happens in during a "normal" day for you? Write about what you do and where you go. Write why you do what you do, and if you enjoy how you spend your time.

Write for a minimum of 10 minutes. Set a timer, then come back to the next prompt.

<Write for 10 minutes>

Now write about the circumstances that led you to this career choice, this relationship, or how you chose to live in your city or region. Trace back to the reasons you made those decisions, and why those priorities worked for you at the time.

<Write for 10 minutes>

What if you did something different for one day? What would you do, and where would you go? Write as if you had no responsibilities and didn't have to answer to anyone. Write whatever pops into your head without judging whether you "should" be thinking that, and without planning how you could actually achieve that in real life. This is a writing exercise, so go ahead and let your imagination run wild!

<Write for 10 minutes, then come back>

Creative writing is drawing a bit upon your known reality, then making up a new story. What story do you want to tell with your life?

Lighten Up

This is not about acting happy when you're not. This is about letting go.

Do you carry any burdens from the past? What thoughts nag you in your quiet moments? What do you wish you could stop remembering?

<Make a short list>

If you could change the feeling that goes with that memory, would you be able to keep the lesson from the event?

<Write for five minutes>

What do you want to remember, and what do you want to let go of?

Try writing for 10 minutes, and keep writing until the

timer goes off. Let one thing lead to another, and enjoy the feeling of the keys under your fingers. You are free to write whatever you want.

<Write for 10 minutes>

What's the Worst That Could Happen?

What are some fears or anxieties that sometimes pop into your head?

<Make a list>

Look back over your list, and choose your worst fear.

If the worst thing actually did happen, what would it do to your life? And what would that mean about you?

<Write for seven minutes>

If you did survive that worst thing happening, how would you change? Would there be any positive effects from the experience?

<Write for five minutes>

Are you still fearful of that thing happening? Why or why not?

<Write for five minutes>

THE Outfit

What is your favorite piece of clothing to wear? If it kept you comfortable in any weather condition and made you feel great, what outfit or item would that be? Mentally go through your closet, or bring to mind a standout memory, and point the camera back to at yourself. What are you wearing?

<Jot down a brief note about that>

Is there something about the color, the fit, or the way it feels on your body? Bring to mind exactly what makes you excellent in that outfit. Make a few more notes about it.

<Write that out now briefly>

What would you wear in public if you didn't feel self-conscious, and no one could comment on it?

<Set the timer and write for at least five minutes, then come back to this>

Did you imagine the same clothing items, or was it two completely different looks? Were other people's opinions important to you? If your outfits were different, which of the two best represents your personality and attitude?

<Write for five minutes>

Now imagine this signature look as your "superhero" costume. If you had special powers to go with your costume, what would they be?

<Freewrite for at least five minutes, set the timer, then come back to this>

Let's imagine that you could feel awesome no matter what you were wearing. In fact, imagine your superhero powers had nothing whatsoever to do with your costume. They were with you no matter what, every day. What kind of things would you be able to accomplish?

<Write for at least five minutes>

Do you feel powerful and capable now? Describe what you want to accomplish as the "superhero you" in street clothes.

<Write for 10 minutes>

Shoes or Barefoot?

Are you right-handed? Kick off your right shoe only. Wiggle your toes, feel your foot on the floor underneath, and take a few deep breaths.

Let that sensation travel up to your brain and just observe the feeling.

Now notice your other foot, still in its shoe. Feel how that feels, and try not to assign any judgment to that feeling (no should or shouldn't, right or wrong.) Just observe, as if you're watching a movie and have no influence on what happens.

Breathe.

Bring your attention back to those two feet. When you are ready, return your pen to paper and freewrite for 10 minutes.

Who am I without shoes?

<Write for 10 minutes>

I Really Should...

What do you tell yourself you "should" be doing? Jot down your list.

<Write for two minutes>

Look over your list, and underline anything that creates a strong negative strong emotional reaction. Choose the thing that makes you feel the most guilty or anxious.

Now write out all the reasons you believe you should be doing that anxiety-producing thing.

<Write for five minutes>

Next, insert the original "should" thought into this sentence: "If I really wanted to, I could_____"

<Rewrite the sentence using the formula>

When you re-read that sentence now, do you feel you want to do it?

<Simply write your answer: yes or no>

If you answered yes, write about how you will feel after accomplishing it.

If you answered no, write about who you would be without that thought hanging over your head.

<Write for five minutes>

The last prompt is to answer this question: "Now I will..."

<Write for seven minutes>

Changing Direction

If you were doing what you really wanted to do in your spare time, what would that look like? Maybe you do a little of it now, but you want more. Or maybe you've only thought about it.

Now imagine yourself in an empty room. There's only you inside, and that THING you want to do. How much room would it take up? Do you need special equipment? What would it cost to invest in the right supplies? Do you need natural light or specific task lighting? Do you need a desk, a bench, or something altogether different? Do you even need a room, or is it somewhere else?

Spend 10 minutes now, and write about it in detail. Once you have that done, come back here for your next instruction.

<Write for 10 minutes>

<Okay, did you really write something down? If so, then read on....>

Now that you have imagined the perfect set-up for your spare time, how does it feel to finally have everything you need? Write about that for five minutes. Let your anticipation pour onto the page. If you aren't excited or happy about having your place, go back to the beginning and start again. Feel free to write whatever you want, not what other people have told you to do.

<Write for five minutes>

What if you could actually spend some time in that room? If you had just 33 minutes, would it be enough to start? How much time do you need? (A famous prolific writer, Eugene Schwartz, always blocked 33 minutes of writing time to encourage himself to focus, and to have a clear deadline.)

Is there anything else standing between you and the door to that place? (The obstacle might be either a real object or person, or an attitude or belief you have about yourself.)

<Write for 10 minutes>

Now spend some time imagining being in that place, and doing that thing you really want to do. Write about what happens, and why it's important to you. Spend just five minutes writing about that.

<Write for five minutes>

Now with that written down, do you want to make this happen in a real and physical way? Or is it satisfying enough to experience your wants only in writing? What do you want to do next, if anything?

<Write for seven minutes>

Travel in Time

Where were you three years ago? Where did you live, work, and play? Who did you spend time with? How did you carry yourself, what did you wear, how did you feel about your life? Describe that in freewriting.

<Write for seven minutes>

Now think about your life today...how the people and places have changed or stayed the same. Observe today's emotional state. How do you feel right now; are there any mental tapes you play in your head or recurring thoughts you have? Write about your current attitude and outlook.

<Write for five minutes>

Despite the fact that we only have this present moment, let's do an experiment. Think about everything you want to have in your life three years in the future. Write about it now.

<Write for seven minutes>

Did any of your ideas about your future surprise you? Do they excite you? Write about it.

\<Write for three minutes\>

Now imagine as you sleep tonight, all the problems in your life somehow vanish. All your challenges are resolved. Since this happened overnight, you haven't yet realized you're living a new life. When you wake up, what will be different? How will you notice the absence of resistance in your life? Write about it.

\<Write for five minutes\>

Now that you are free to move forward without those restrictions of the past, how will you walk? Will your facial expression be different now that your challenges are resolved? Write about your new feelings of confidence.

\<Write for seven minutes\>

What Would You Do?

If you knew you had the support of your friends and family as well as unlimited resources, what would you create? If you knew you would not fail and your results would be even better than your vision, what would you do?

<Write for 10 minutes>

Dream Your Memories

Do you remember your dreams? I usually can if I let myself linger in that near-awake state. If there are noises in the house or my husband talks to me, they usually go POOF!

Why do you think we dream? Are they merely "brain dumps" of information, off-loading yesterday's events? Are they messages from the deepest parts of ourselves, or messages from other people, places, or times?

Write down what you know and believe about dreaming, and when (or if) you remember your own dreams. Set the timer for five minutes and just freewrite without editing, letting your thoughts pour out onto the page.

<Write for five minutes>

If you could direct your dreams to make something happen, what would you do or feel while dreaming? Would you fly, visit faraway lands, or see someone special? Think of some experiences you'd like to have while dreaming, and write about them.

<Write for seven minutes>

Place a notebook and a pencil by your bed tonight. When you wake from dreaming, a pencil writes easily in the dark. Keep a clipboard or open spiral notebook next to the bed so you can easily reach over and write without fully awakening. Try this for the next three nights, and see where you can go in your dreams.

Having Fun

When was the last time you REALLY had fun, and what did you do? Write about it.

\<Write for seven minutes\>

How was it to write about those feelings?

\<Write for three minutes\>

Jot a quick list of what you need more of in your life.

\<Write for one minute\>

How (or why) will getting what you need make your life better, happier, or more full? What do you need to stop saying to yourself so that you can get more of what you need? What thoughts can you let go of?

\<Write for seven minutes\>

Defining Ourselves

What is your opinion of creativity? If someone pursues art, writing, or music, what kind of person are they?

<Write for five minutes>

How do you feel about calling yourself a creative person? What would happen if you claimed the label of artist, musician, or writer? What would that give you permission to do next?

<Write for ten minutes>

If My Dreams Came True, I Would...

What is something that you really, REALLY want to do, but you don't think you can?

\<Write for five minutes>

Why can't you do it?

\<Write for two minutes>

What conditions would have to change for you to be able to do that? What would you have to do differently?

\<Write for five minutes>

What help or support would you need to change your conditions?

\<Write for five minutes>

What is one small thing you could do each day to move you closer to your dreams?

<Write for two minutes>

Use this formula to check your idea:

By doing _____ (the one small thing each day,) I will create _____ (your dream come true.)

Does this formula work for you, or is something still missing? What would make the formula work?

<Write for five minutes>

Special Delivery Envelope

Remember to take this idea and let yourself freewrite about it. Don't stop to edit, just let one thought lead to another on the page.

Suppose you received notice that something amazing was about to happen... You will be given an eighth day in your week. The rest of the world will be on "pause," and no one will know they're missing anything. This phenomenon will re-occur for one month, and will never happen again. What will you do with your extra day each week?

\<Write for ten minutes>

What Color Are Your Eyes?

Imagine yourself standing in front of your bathroom mirror. Look at your hair, your face, and your eyes. *Really* look – see your eye color and the depth of your gaze. Notice how you feel. Take a moment to imagine that now. As you're making that deep intimate connection with yourself in the mirror, say "I am willing to change."

Notice how you feel in your body, and what comes into your head. Let those feelings have time to express themselves to you. When you're ready, freewrite about it. Let one thought lead to another, and just write without stopping. This is for your eyes only.

<Write for five minutes>

What did you find out about yourself? What did you feel about the prospect of change?

<Write for five minutes>

Me? A Character?

If you were the main character in a book, what kind of plot twists would show your true nature? How different is the "real you" from the one you reveal to others? Freewrite about the protected parts of you that are too precious to share with anyone else.

\<Write for ten minutes>

Truth is Stranger than Fiction

If you could now use those most precious parts of your life as a work of fiction, what would your book be titled? Write down 10 possibilities. Make them as wild and weird as needed to come up with 10 titles.

<Write down 10 possible book titles>

Look back over those titles, and choose the one you like the most.

If you actually wrote a fictional novel with that title and used a pen name as the author, how would it feel to tell the real story of you?

<Write for ten minutes>

What's Next?

Let's talk about your story and the book you really want to write. I'd like to know more, and see how I can support your big writing dream. Let's set up a 30 minute project discussion, and put together a plan for your book! You can choose the best time for your schedule with this link: www.timetrade.com/book/LT7VG, or send an email to my personal inbox: cjyoung@fuse.net.

If this book was helpful, will you please review it on my Amazon Author page? Five stars is most appreciated along with one sentence of how this helped. Your review may be the exact thing the next aspiring author needs to hear! Search Amazon.com under Christina Young, or type this short link into your web browser: https://amzn.to/2AhFc0q (this is case sensitive and that is a zero before the q ☺) Thank you for spending your time with my book. Now let's talk about your book idea!

About the Author

Christina Dreve Young coaches aspiring authors to complete their first draft in thirty days. In a small group program called "Get Your Book Started", she helps you outline fiction, non-fiction, memoir, or your business book. Christina provides the framework and support that allows you to finally tell your story. With just thirty minutes of daily writing time, you can not only start your book, but also complete your manuscript in one month.

Find out more at www.GetYourBookStarted.com. Want to receive a new writing prompt every week? Join the *Tuesday Writing Club* at www.GetYourBookStarted.com.

If you'd like to talk with Christina about your book, schedule a free thirty minute project discussion by copying this link: www.timetrade.com/book/LT7VG

Christina lives with her husband Glen, and their little pets Chica and Pickles in their five-acre woods east of Cincinnati, Ohio.

www.ingramcontent.com/pod-product-compliance
Lightning Source LLC
Chambersburg PA
CBHW051035030426
42336CB00015B/2884